W9-AAT-474

STEM IN THE REAL WORLD

FORENSICS
IN THE REAL WORLD

by L. E. Carmichael

Content Consultant
Claire Glynn, PhD
Assistant Professor, Department of Forensic Science
University of New Haven

Core Library

An Imprint of Abdo Publishing
abdopublishing.com

abdopublishing.com

Published by Abdo Publishing, a division of ABDO, PO Box 398166, Minneapolis, Minnesota 55439. Copyright © 2017 by Abdo Consulting Group, Inc. International copyrights reserved in all countries. No part of this book may be reproduced in any form without written permission from the publisher. Core Library™ is a trademark and logo of Abdo Publishing.

Printed in the United States of America, North Mankato, Minnesota
082016
012017

 THIS BOOK CONTAINS
RECYCLED MATERIALS

Cover Photo: Anthony Devlin/PA Wire URN:12393849/AP Images
Interior Photos: Anthony Devlin/PA Wire URN:12393849/AP Images, 1; Ivan Bliznetsov/iStockphoto, 4; Paolo Cipriani/iStockphoto, 6; Richard T. Nowitz/Science Source, 10, 31, 34, 43; iStockphoto, 14; Red Line Editorial, 17, 37; Mauro Fermariello/Science Source, 21, 45; Taylor Irby/Jackson Citizen Patriot-Mlive.com/AP Images, 24; Andrew Vaughan/CP Photo/AP Images, 28; Peter Menzel/Science Source, 32; Pascal Goetgheluck/Science Source, 40

Editor: Arnold Ringstad
Series Designer: Ryan Gale

Publisher's Cataloging-in-Publication Data

Names: Carmichael, L. E., author.
Title: Forensics the real world / by L. E. Carmichael.
Description: Minneapolis, MN : Abdo Publishing, 2017. | Series: STEM in the real
    world | Includes bibliographical references and index.
Identifiers: LCCN 2016945442 | ISBN 9781680784794 (lib. bdg.) |
    ISBN 9781680798647 (ebook)
Subjects: LCSH: Forensic genetics--Juvenile literature. | DNA fingerprinting--
    Juvenile literature. | DNA analysis--Juvenile literature. | Forensic science--
    Juvenile literature.
Classification: DDC 614--dc23
LC record available at http://lccn.loc.gov/2016945442

CONTENTS

CHAPTER ONE

WHAT IS FORENSICS?

It was 1988. In the town of Narborough, England, two teenage girls had been murdered. Police thought Richard Buckland was guilty. But they had no proof. They turned to a new breakthrough in forensics for help.

Officers called Alec Jeffreys, a scientist from a local university. Jeffreys studied genetics, the science of DNA. DNA is found in the skin, muscle, blood,

Forensic scientists carefully collect evidence from crime scenes.

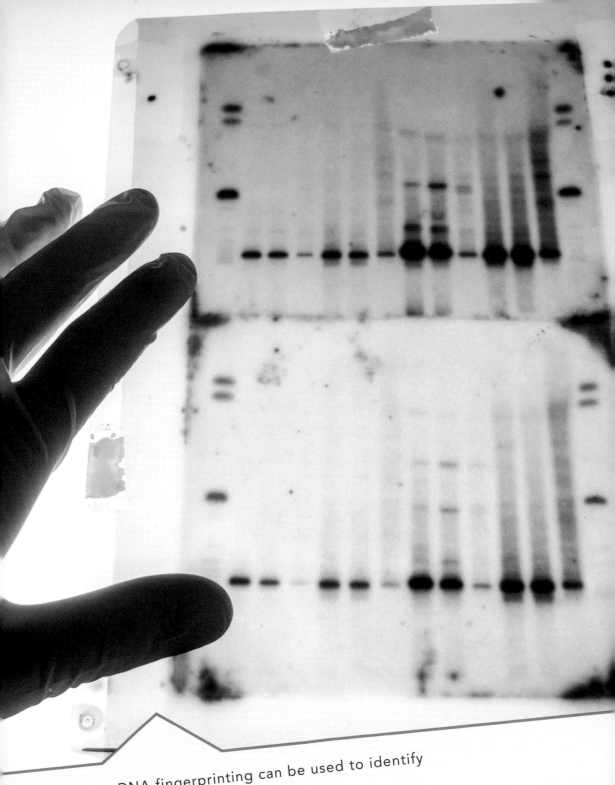

DNA fingerprinting can be used to identify specific people.

bone, teeth, and hair of animals, including humans. It contains the instructions for making living things.

Every person's DNA is 99.9 percent identical to every other person's. Jeffreys wanted to find the parts of DNA that differ. One day he tried a new experiment on DNA from three people. The results were amazing. Each person's DNA formed a pattern of lines. Each pattern was unique. Jeffreys realized his discovery could be used to identify people. He called it DNA fingerprinting.

Narborough police had read about Jeffreys's experiment. They asked him to test DNA evidence found on the bodies of the victims. Jeffreys proved that the DNA from both crime scenes matched. This meant that the same man had killed both girls. Next Jeffreys compared DNA from the crime scene with DNA from Buckland's blood. The patterns differed. Buckland was innocent.

Police had faith in the new science. But they had no other suspects. They asked people to donate

IN THE REAL WORLD

DNA: Past and Present

DNA fingerprinting has greatly improved over the last 30 years. In the past, the test required blood smears the size of a dime. Today scientists can fingerprint the DNA in a single hair. In the past, only fresh DNA samples could be tested. Today DNA evidence solves crimes that took place more than 40 years ago.

American crime labs test more than 1 million DNA samples per year. Some come from crime scenes. The rest come from known criminals. These DNA fingerprints help police link people to crimes.

blood and saliva for testing. More than 4,500 men volunteered. But scientists could not find a match to the killer. Then police heard a rumor. Colin Pitchfork had never donated blood. He had paid a friend to give blood in his name. Police arrested Pitchfork. They tested his DNA. It was a perfect match to the DNA from the murders. On January 23, 1988, Pitchfork went to prison for life. Science had cracked the case.

The Science of Crime

Forensics is possible because "every contact leaves a trace." This idea comes from pioneering forensic scientist Edmond Locard. It is known as Locard's Exchange Principle. It means that when a person commits a crime, he or she leaves evidence. That evidence is physical. It is real. It can be searched for, identified, and interpreted by forensic scientists.

Forensic scientists called crime scene investigators (CSIs) search for evidence. Different crimes produce different types of evidence.

Edmond Locard

French scientist Edmond Locard loved Sherlock Holmes stories. This fictional detective often solved crimes using the tiniest of clues. Locard believed dust, ash, hair, and threads could be important evidence in real life too.

At the time, many police departments thought he was crazy. Locard did not care. He opened his own crime lab in 1910. Soon he was using tiny clues to solve cases. Today tiny evidence is known as trace evidence. Studying these clues is an important part of forensic science.

Major police departments have their own large DNA labs.

DNA is one type. Paint chips, bullets, fingerprints, drugs, and even dust can also be important clues. CSIs know where to look for evidence. They also know how to safely transport it to the lab.

At the lab, forensic specialists study the evidence. Sometimes they look at it. Sometimes they perform scientific tests. Often they try to match unknown samples from crime scenes to samples from victims or suspects. Because there are many types of evidence, forensic specialists use many types of science.

Based on the evidence, specialists try to figure out what happened. This is called reconstructing the crime. Forensic scientists share their results with police, who arrest the criminals. Later, scientists share their results in court. This is called expert testimony. Their testimony brings criminals to justice. Many cases can be solved only with the help of forensic science.

The Truth

Careers in forensics are exciting. But they carry a lot of responsibility. Crime science is important work that has to be done correctly. Mistakes could mean that innocent people go to jail. Mistakes could also free guilty people. Then they would be able to commit more crimes. Good forensic scientists have knowledge and skills. They gain these skills through training and experience. They believe in using facts to find the truth.

Paul Kirk specialized in reconstructing crimes from bloodstains. This excerpt is from Kirk's forensic how-to book, *Crime Investigation*:

> *Wherever he steps, whatever he touches, whatever he leaves, even unconsciously, will serve as silent witness against him. Not only his fingerprints or his footprints, but his hair, the fibers from his clothes, the glass he breaks, the tool marks he leaves, the paint he scratches, the blood . . . he deposits or collects—All of these and more bear mute witness against him. This is evidence that does not forget. It is not confused by the excitement of the moment. It is not absent because human witnesses are. It cannot perjure itself; it cannot be wholly absent. Only its interpretation can err. Only human failure to find it, study and understand it, can diminish its value.*

Source: Paul L. Kirk. Crime Investigation.
2nd ed. New York: John Wiley & Sons, 1974. Print. 2.

Consider Your Audience

Review this passage closely. Consider how you would adapt it for a different audience, such as your parents, your principal, or younger friends. Write a blog post conveying this same information for the new audience. What is the most effective way to get your point across to this audience? How does your new approach differ from the original text, and why?

CHAPTER TWO

THE HISTORY OF FORENSICS

Someone has died, and police are suspicious. Was the death natural, accidental, or a murder? To find out, forensic scientists perform an autopsy. They study the body inside and out. They look for evidence of a crime.

Roman doctor Antistius did the first autopsy of a murder victim in 44 BCE. The leader of Rome,

The murder of Julius Caesar led to one early use of forensic science.

Julius Caesar, had been stabbed 23 times. Antistius looked at each wound. He found one that pierced the heart. The man who made this wound had killed Caesar.

Autopsy is the oldest branch of forensics, but the science of autopsies was slow to improve. That is because it was once a crime to cut open a dead body. European countries made autopsy legal in the 1400s and 1500s. After the 1500s, doctors had bodies to practice on. They quickly learned to recognize the signs of murder.

Knife and bullet wounds were easy to identify. Poison was much harder. Murderers utilized a poison called arsenic. It was used to kill rats. Arsenic was cheap and easy to buy. It had no taste or smell. People dying of arsenic appeared to have cholera, a common disease at the time.

To prove poisoning, scientists needed to find arsenic inside the victim. This was difficult. Early experiments turned the poison into a gas. The gas

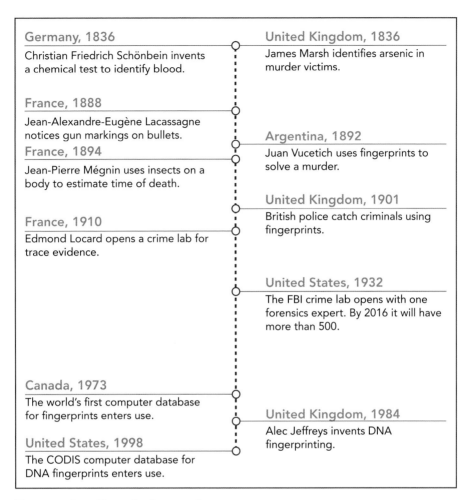

Germany, 1836
Christian Friedrich Schönbein invents a chemical test to identify blood.

United Kingdom, 1836
James Marsh identifies arsenic in murder victims.

France, 1888
Jean-Alexandre-Eugène Lacassagne notices gun markings on bullets.

Argentina, 1892
Juan Vucetich uses fingerprints to solve a murder.

France, 1894
Jean-Pierre Mégnin uses insects on a body to estimate time of death.

United Kingdom, 1901
British police catch criminals using fingerprints.

France, 1910
Edmond Locard opens a crime lab for trace evidence.

United States, 1932
The FBI crime lab opens with one forensics expert. By 2016 it will have more than 500.

Canada, 1973
The world's first computer database for fingerprints enters use.

United Kingdom, 1984
Alec Jeffreys invents DNA fingerprinting.

United States, 1998
The CODIS computer database for DNA fingerprints enters use.

Forensics Breakthroughs

Many forensic methods were invented in Europe during the 1800s. The Industrial Revolution took place around the same time. Why would the Industrial Revolution increase the need for forensic science?

escaped before it could be identified. Then, in 1836, James Marsh invented a way to collect arsenic. In his device, the trapped gas formed a black stain. During trials, jurors could see this stain. They started sending poisoners to prison.

Criminals and Crime Scenes

Murder is messy. The victim's blood often gets on a killer's clothes. Therefore, bloodstains are strong evidence. But murderers could once claim that bloodstains came from hunted animals. There was no way to know who was lying.

German scientist Paul Uhlenhuth solved this problem in 1901. He added a rabbit's blood to human blood. The mixture got clumpy. When Uhlenhuth mixed rabbit blood with animal blood, nothing happened. Uhlenhuth soon solved a murder with his powerful test.

In the United Kingdom, scientists found another way to connect people with their crimes: fingerprints. Human fingers are covered with ridges. The shapes of these ridges are unique to each individual person. They do not change over a person's life.

Along the ridges, microscopic pores ooze oil and sweat. This ooze gets left behind on things we touch. It creates latent fingerprints. British scientists used inks and powders to make latent prints visible. Then Edward Henry grouped fingerprint patterns into arches, loops, and whorls. That made it easy to compare prints. British police launched Henry's system in 1901. The following year, they caught 1,500 criminals using fingerprints.

If fingerprints could be matched to fingers, could bullets be matched

IN THE REAL WORLD
Looking Closer

Comparison microscopes are helpful in forensics. These devices magnify two items at once. They show the images side by side. That makes it easier to see if the items match.

Russian scientist Alexander von Inostranzeff invented the comparison microscope in 1885. These devices became popular after Calvin Goddard used one to solve the Saint Valentine's Day Massacre. Today comparison microscopes are connected to screens. That makes the images even bigger.

to guns? Calvin Goddard thought so. The Saint Valentine's Day Massacre of 1929 gave him a chance to prove it. On February 14, men in police uniforms entered a warehouse in Chicago, Illinois, and started shooting. They killed seven people, including five who worked for a gangster named "Bugs" Moran. The city was outraged. Police asked Goddard to prove their innocence.

Goddard compared bullets from the warehouse with bullets from police guns. The markings on the shells were different. That meant the shooters were not really police. According to the evidence, they may have worked for rival gangster Al Capone. The case became famous. Thanks to Goddard's work, ballistics became an important forensic science.

Forensics Today

Modern forensics is based on these and other historical methods. Two major breakthroughs have happened in recent times. One is DNA fingerprinting. The other is computers.

Forensic scientists can use computers to recreate three-dimensional images of crime scenes.

Computers entered use in some forensics labs in the 1960s. Scientists used them to store fingerprints, ballistics data, and other kinds of evidence. Today computers search for matches. Then scientists check their results. This is much faster than doing the whole job by hand. For example, police in Los Angeles,

California, had 1.7 million fingerprint records in 1984. In minutes, their new computer matched a murderer's print to prints from a known criminal. A forensic scientist would have needed 67 years to do the same thing.

A New Kind of Evidence

Before the 1980s, most people could not afford to own computers. Today people use them to commit crimes that did not exist 40 years ago. Hacking, identity theft, and piracy are only a few examples.

Digital forensics is the science of computer crime. It is the fastest growing branch of forensics. It is also very difficult. Technology changes constantly. Digital detectives work hard to keep up with computer criminals.

Digital forensics is another modern field. Many people commit crimes using computers and the Internet. They may break into bank websites and steal money. They may harass people online. They may buy or sell drugs using their cell phones. Digital forensics experts can track criminals on the Internet. They link criminals to their digital crimes.

Calvin Goddard studied bullets from the Saint Valentine's Day Massacre. He proved that police did not commit the crime. Later, he matched the bullets to a gun owned by a gangster who worked for Al Capone. This excerpt is from a paper Goddard published about the case:

> Since it is not possible, no matter how careful the effort, to produce any two gun parts exactly alike (though they are easily made enough alike to be interchangeable) it follows that each part that comes in contact with a shell will have certain individual characteristics which it can imprint upon the softer metal of that shell, thereby leaving upon it a signature, as it were. Two shells bearing the identical "signature" must necessarily have been fired in the same gun.

> Source: Calvin Goddard. "The Valentine Day Massacre: A Study in Ammunition-Tracing." The American Journal of Police Science 1.1 (1930): 60–78. Print. 67.

What's the Big Idea?

Take a close look at this passage. What is Goddard saying about how guns are made? How does a gun affect the bullets it fires? Why is this so important for forensics?

CAREERS IN FORENSICS

Forensics is a fast-growing field. Because of television crime shows, it is also very popular. A lot of people compete for a small number of jobs. Students who want to work in forensics need to prepare. They should take math and science classes in high school. Before applying to a university, they should research what kinds of forensic careers sound most interesting to them.

Students in school and at science camps can begin working on their forensics skills.

Crime Scene Investigators

CSIs find and collect evidence at crime scenes. But first they sketch and photograph the entire area. It is important to record the location of every piece of evidence. This helps to reconstruct the crime.

CSIs look, listen, and even sniff for clues. They decide which details could explain what happened. CSIs place evidence in jars, bags, or boxes. They search for latent evidence, such as fingerprints or DNA samples. CSIs must be thorough but quick. At outdoor crime scenes, bad weather could destroy evidence.

IN THE REAL WORLD

The *CSI* Effect

Much of the science on television crime shows, such as *CSI*, is exaggerated or false. Many jurors do not know that. They believe that forensics in the real world works the way it does on television. They expect forensic evidence in every trial. They expect crime scene reconstructions to be 100 percent accurate. This has created a problem. CSIs know that jurors want forensics. They often collect so much evidence that crime labs cannot keep up.

Murder investigations include a second crime scene: the victim. CSIs take all evidence involving the victim to the crime lab for study. Finally, they write down what they saw and did. These reports help if CSIs are asked to speak about the case in court.

CSIs must be ready to work whenever a crime is committed. They often miss sleep or fun with friends and family. The work is dirty, smelly, and challenging. At a large scene, CSIs may work several days without rest. They must be able to crouch or kneel for hours. They sometimes have to lift heavy objects. The hardest part of the job, though, is seeing the effects of violent crimes. CSIs must stay calm when surrounded by death and destruction.

To become a CSI, a person must first earn a bachelor's degree in science. He or she may also join a police force. Most CSIs are police officers who later train in crime scene investigation. Others do their forensics work outside of police forces.

Crime scenes are blocked off and evidence is carefully tracked so CSIs can do their work.

Forensic Specialists

Forensic specialists work in crime labs. They use microscopes to look at evidence. They identify unknown substances. They match evidence to victims or suspects. Using all this information, specialists reconstruct the crime.

Most forensic specialists are experts in a single type of evidence. Some focus on DNA fingerprinting. Some compare bullets or use chemistry to identify poisons and drugs. Others do autopsies or study insects. Expert knowledge requires extra education. After earning their bachelor's degrees, many specialists get a master's degree or PhD. They also train with experienced scientists before handling evidence on their own. Forensic specialists

Training with Toys

Frances Glessner Lee loved forensics and worried that police did not understand it. In the 1940s, she came up with an unusual solution: dollhouses. Lee built detailed miniature crime scenes filled with tiny clues. She called them the "Nutshell Studies of Unexplained Death." Police used these models to practice investigating crimes. Forensic evidence was the key to each mystery.

Lee became an honorary police captain. She was also the first female member of the American Academy of Forensic Sciences. People can see her "Nutshell Studies" at the medical examiner's office in Baltimore, Maryland.

improve their knowledge and skills throughout their careers.

Specialists must be patient and meticulous. Bloodstain experts may spend an entire day looking for droplets on a pair of black shoes. Curiosity and problem-solving skills are also very important. When reconstructing crimes, specialists must choose between several possible explanations. For example, is a suspect's DNA on a knife handle because she is a murderer or because she chopped vegetables?

Specialists must be organized. They may work on up to 30 cases at once. Communication skills are also important. Forensic specialists write reports, describing their results for police. In court, specialists explain forensic science clearly so that jurors can understand it. To become a forensic specialist, people should study their favorite type of science. Then they should apply for a job at a city or state crime lab.

Some forensic researchers study how analyzing bullets can help identify guns.

Forensic Researchers

Researchers do experiments in forensic science. They help CSIs and specialists understand how crimes create evidence. They make current forensic methods more accurate. They invent new ways to solve crimes. Alec Jeffreys was doing research when he invented DNA fingerprinting. Other researchers look for better ways to estimate a victim's time of death. Others splash blood on hard and soft surfaces to study how the shapes of the drops change.

Forensics students learn how to find and analyze bodies.

Only 7 percent of crime labs hire forensic
researchers. Most of these are large labs, such as the
one at the FBI. Researchers usually work at colleges
and universities. Students do experiments to earn a
master's degree or PhD. Professors who teach forensic
science also do research.

Following the Evidence

Some universities offer special degrees in forensics.
But professional forensic scientists suggest picking

a natural science field, such as biology or chemistry. They say it is important to remember that forensic science is a science. Forensic scientists should have a very good knowledge of physics, chemistry, biology, and mathematics.

Lab workers may face stress. Sometimes police might have a suspect in mind. They may pressure scientists to prove that a suspect committed the crime. Forensic scientists must be brave enough to follow the evidence, no matter where it leads.

FURTHER EVIDENCE

Chapter Three describes careers in forensic science. What is one of the main points of this chapter? What evidence does the author use to support this point? Read the article at the website below. Does this article support the evidence in the chapter? What new evidence does it add?

Cool Jobs: Crime Scene Investigators

mycorelibrary.com/forensics

CHAPTER FOUR

THE FUTURE OF FORENSICS

James Marsh invented a test for arsenic. Murderers switched to other poisons. Edward Henry collected fingerprints. Criminals started wearing gloves. Paul Uhlenhuth identified blood. Killers cleaned up. Over time, criminals have learned to hide the evidence.

This is why forensic research is so important. It helps scientists stay one step ahead of the criminals.

Light sources can be used to reveal the presence of blood and other fluids.

Luminol is a great example. Developed in the 1930s, luminol is a chemical that reacts with blood. The reaction produces light. Luminol can find one drop of blood mixed with 10,000 drops of water. No matter how well criminals clean up, crime scenes will still glow in the dark.

Future Forensics

Today's research becomes tomorrow's science. For example, there are two ways to identify someone from his or her DNA. Using a database, scientists match crime scene DNA to that of a known criminal. Or they match crime scene DNA to a known suspect. But what if police have no suspects?

It is now possible to draw pictures of criminals based on crime scene DNA. The process works because pieces of DNA called genes affect the way people look. By examining the genes for hair color, eye color, face shape, and skin tone, scientists create images of unknown suspects. The pictures are then compared with actual people. More research will be

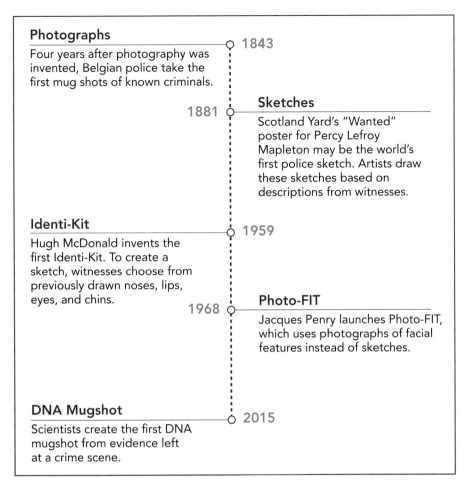

Photographs

Four years after photography was invented, Belgian police take the first mug shots of known criminals.

1843

1881

Sketches

Scotland Yard's "Wanted" poster for Percy Lefroy Mapleton may be the world's first police sketch. Artists draw these sketches based on descriptions from witnesses.

Identi-Kit

Hugh McDonald invents the first Identi-Kit. To create a sketch, witnesses choose from previously drawn noses, lips, eyes, and chins.

1959

1968

Photo-FIT

Jacques Penry launches Photo-FIT, which uses photographs of facial features instead of sketches.

DNA Mugshot

Scientists create the first DNA mugshot from evidence left at a crime scene.

2015

The Evolving Face of Crime

When it comes to identifying criminals, art is just as important as science. Forensic artists use several methods to capture a criminal's face. How accurate are these methods? What are their advantages and disadvantages?

needed before this method can be used in court. But someday it may be a powerful forensic tool.

Other researchers think bacteria could help identify suspects. Bacteria are microscopic creatures

Estimating Time of Death

In murder cases, when someone died is just as important as how. After all, a suspect who was busy at the time of the crime cannot be the killer. Time of death is one of the hardest questions for science to answer. Thanks to William Bass, it is getting easier.

In 1980 Bass opened the "body farm" at the University of Tennessee. People donate their bodies to science after death. Bass places the bodies in sunshine, in car trunks, or underwater. Then he watches the bodies change over time. These experiments have made time of death estimates much more accurate.

that live on the human body. Every person's mix of bacteria types may be unique. When we breathe out, shed hairs, or touch things, bacteria transfer to our surroundings. In the future, scientists may be able to catch criminals using the bacteria they leave behind.

Bacteria could also help scientists pinpoint time of death. When a person dies, the immune system stops working. Instantly, bacteria in the body begin multiplying. Bacterial growth changes human bodies in specific ways. With today's methods, forensic scientists can measure time of death within a couple of days. Bacteria evidence could narrow those estimates to a few hours.

Solving Tomorrow's Crimes

Each new discovery offers a new way to solve crimes. But forensic evidence is only as good as the scientists who find and study it. Lazy, careless, or unethical scientists could let criminals get away with murder. They may let more good people get hurt.

The Innocence Project

Whether accidental or deliberate, mistakes in the criminal justice system can have serious consequences. Thousands of innocent people are in jail because of bad science.

The Innocence Project began in 1992. Its goal is to use DNA fingerprinting to free those who have been wrongfully convicted. By 2016 the Innocence Project had helped more than 300 people regain their freedom. In more than 140 of those cases, the real criminal was also found.

Today's forensic scientists use sophisticated tools to help solve crimes.

- Good forensic scientists are willing to work hard to find the truth and follow the evidence wherever it leads.
- DNA fingerprinting has made it possible to identify more criminals from the evidence they leave behind.
- Computers have become crucial tools for forensic scientists of all kinds.

STOP AND THINK

Surprise Me

Chapter One explains how DNA fingerprinting helped solve the Colin Pitchfork case. What two or three facts about this case were most surprising? Write a few sentences about each fact. Why did these facts surprise you?

Dig Deeper

After reading this book, what questions do you still have about forensics? Ask an adult to help you find reliable sources of information on forensic science. Write a short paragraph describing the answers you find.

Say What?

Scientists use special vocabulary to describe their work. Find five words in this book you have never heard before. Look them up in a dictionary. Write their meanings in your own words. Then try using each word in a new sentence.

You Are There

Imagine you are helping Calvin Goddard solve the Saint Valentine's Day Massacre. Write a short report describing your investigation. Talk about the evidence you study and what kinds of clues you look for. Be sure to use lots of detail.

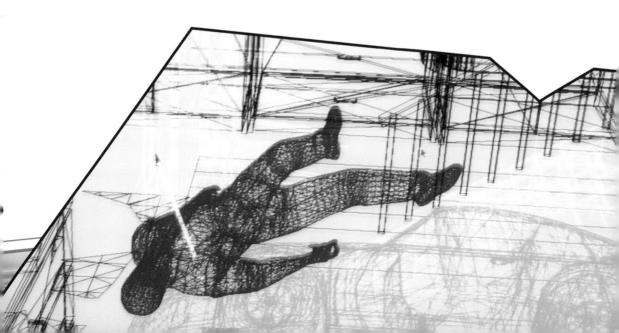

GLOSSARY

ballistics
the study of guns and bullets

hacking
breaking into someone's computer

identity theft
stealing someone's name, usually to take their money or property

immune system
natural defenses that protect the body from bacteria and viruses

jurors
ordinary people who attend trials and must decide, based on evidence, whether an accused person is guilty or innocent

latent
evidence that is present but not visible

piracy
stealing information, such as songs, books, or movies, off the Internet

pores
tiny openings in the skin that allow oil and sweat to escape the body

shell
the casing of a bullet that falls off when a gun is fired

testimony
statements that witnesses and experts make in court during a trial

LEARN MORE

Books

Carmichael, L. E. *Fuzzy Forensics: DNA Fingerprinting Gets Wild.* Halifax, Nova Scotia: Alopex Editions, 2015.

Hamilton, Sue. *How to Become a Crime Scene Investigator.* Minneapolis, MN: Abdo Publishing, 2008.

Townsend, John. *Forensic Secrets.* Mankato, MN: Amicus, 2012.

Websites

To learn more about STEM in the Real World, visit **booklinks.abdopublishing.com**. These links are routinely monitored and updated to provide the most current information available.

Visit **mycorelibrary.com** for free additional tools for teachers and students.

INDEX

ABOUT THE AUTHOR

L. E. Carmichael has published 18 children's science books on everything from scoliosis to hybrid cars. Her book *Fuzzy Forensics: DNA Fingerprinting Gets Wild* won a Lane Anderson Award for exceptional children's science writing.